Fruit 2 Chew

Ebony D. Jefferson

Copyright © 2022 by Ebony D. Jefferson
Fruit2Chew
Conversations.bookings@gmail.com

All rights reserved. In accordance with the U.S. Copyright Act of 1976, the scanning, uploading, and electronic sharing of any part of this book without the permission of the publisher is unlawful piracy and theft of the author's intellectual property. If you would like to use material from the book, prior written permission must be obtained by contacting the publisher at info@entegritypublishing.com
Thank you for your support of the author's rights.

The views expressed in this work are solely those of the author and do not necessarily reflect the views of the publisher, and the publisher hereby disclaims any responsibility for them.
Entegrity Choice Publishing
PO Box 453
Powder Springs, GA 30127
info@entegritypublishing.com
www.entegritypublishing.com
770.727.6517

Printed in the United States of America

Library of Congress Cataloging-in-Publication Data
ISBN 979-8-9850792-2-7

Library of Congress Control Number: 2021925148

Contents

Introduction	7
The Blind Leading the Blind	9
Be Authentically You	10
Take the Risk	11
Measure Up	12
Is the Price Right?	13
Everyone Can't Go	14
Take Control	15
Make Room for Your Next	16
Healing Beyond the Surface	17
Unconditional Love Can't Wait	18
Do What You Can, While You Can	19
Be Great in Every Season	20
Forgive Anyway	21
Your Life Is Already Mapped Out	22
Trust God Through It All	23
Everything Is Working Together for Your Good	24
You Are Enough	25

Seek to First Understand 26
Be Careful How Your Keys Are Used 27
Humility Begins in The Heart. 28
Don't Miss Out 29
Unmask Your Truth 30
Under but Not Buried 31
Positive Words Bring New Life 32
No Matter What, Keep Trying. 33
How Are You Loving Today? 34
Action Speak Louder Than Words. 35
Recalibrate Your Heart. 36
Who Are You? 37
How Are You Evolving? 38
Don't Wait on "Them"Be "YOU" 39
Free Your Mind 40
Who Cares? 41
You Can't Move Forward Walking Backwards 42
Don't Settle 43
Don't Force It 44
He Loves You...Not. 45
No Pretending Here. 46
It Had to Happen This Way 47
Forgiveness Gives You Permission to Live. 48
Keep Shining. 49
Heart of Stone 50
Stay Ready 51
Use What You Got. 52
Be Careful How You Climb 53
Perfectly Imperfect. 54

God Is Worth the Wait 55
But Who Are You in Real Life? 56
Slow Your Roll 57
Value What's In Your Hands 58
Trust 59
They Will Never Understand 60
Processed For Purpose 61
What Matters Most 62
Right Size, Right Packaging 63
Be The TRUE You 64
Blocked and Blessed 65
Best Is Better 68
Break the Chain 69
Let Him Perfect the Work 70
Keep On Moving 71
Make Room 72
Pace Yourself 73
How Is Your View? 74
Let God Upgrade You 75
More than Enough 76
Gift Giver 77
Big Open Door 78
Real Love 79
Who's Calling You? 80
Net Watcher 81
Love Makes Things Happen 82

Introduction

Fruit2Chew was birthed while I was going through one season of the many transitions in my life. It's a collection of ten years of thoughts combined into one body of work that is still relevant today. I want to bless someone with these words as I have been blessed.

I prayed to God every morning about each individual situation I was facing, sometimes begging Him to remove the problem or guide me through it; better yet, I would ask Him why He had me in that place if He wasn't going to move on my behalf. Soon enough, God began to speak to me at random times of the day, and without thought I posted His words on social media. One day, I discovered that God was answering my prayers by giving me snippets of "Fruit," His Word, to chew and digest. I was sitting in my car and He said, "This is Fruit2Chew on, just like you chew on my words."

There are times when God may not take you immediately out of a situation but instead leave you in, allowing you to grow and heal through it, so that when it is over, you will not have any second thoughts or regrets, no matter how hard it gets. In every test or trial, don't disrupt the process. God is Growing you in Grace.

The Blind Leading the Blind

There is nothing worse than listening to a BROKEN person trying to give you suggestions on how to better your life based on something they have read, rather than a life experience they've walked through.

Be Authentically You

You can't expect anyone to be honest with you about their true feelings toward you if they themselves are still wearing a mask, and haven't faced who they really are. Never second-guess who YOU are because of someone else's insecurities. Live and love unapologetically.

Take the Risk

If you handle God's business concerning helping others, then He will surely handle YOUR business concerning YOU. Sometimes what you get is better than what you want.

Measure Up

Know your worth is not measured by how others treat or measure you, but rather by how you treat and measure yourself.

Is the Price Right?

One should never get so caught up in the "feeling" of a thing that they forget the "High Price" they had to pay in their "Then" to get to their "NOW."

Everyone Can't Go

There will come a time in your life that you realize more and more how much you have changed. It was all for *my making*. Realizing that your vision has been sharpened and your level of compassion and patience has increased. It is all working together to create someone great! Continue the path less traveled no matter what. The longer the journey, the less weight I must carry. #EverybodyCan'tGo

Take Control

When you are not willing to heal from the hurt "they" have caused you, will allow "them" to control your life and dictate your emotions even when they are not around. #TakeBackUrControl

Make Room for Your Next

It's okay to close the door permanently. It's not that you don't love them and want God's best for them. But you love you more. Not everyone has the capacity to receive what you have to give. Allow God to make room in your life for what's supposed to be there. If you can't be real with yourself, it is impossible to be real with anyone else...

Healing Beyond the Surface

One should not get so wrapped up in the attention that they receive from telling the "story" that they forget the part that they played in how that "story" ended. True healing comes from being honest and transparent with yourself first.

Unconditional Love Can't Wait

Never become satisfied with the bare minimum when the maximum is available. Love is a choice and must be nurtured daily. Never take real unconditional love for granted; if not embraced or recognized, it may disappear without warning. Time waits for no one.

Do What You Can, While You Can

G ive what you are capable of giving. Handle what your hands have the ability to hold. Love according to your capacity to receive and leave the rest to God.

Be Great in Every Season

The great thing about being authentic and secure with yourself and where you are in the "NOW" season of your life is that you don't have to switch masks depending on the people or the environment that you enter.

Forgive Anyway

The best peace one could have is the ability to honestly forgive someone who hurt you. Forgiveness is not for them but for YOU.

Your Life Is Already Mapped Out

Don't ever feel as though you have to seek validation from others for something that GOD has called YOU to do... There is a reason that YOU were chosen in the first place, so walk in "IT" unapologetically.

Trust God Through It All

God's plan for your life is greater than your own. Work your faith and continue to trust Him during the process. Some folks want to obtain the "Results of God" but aren't willing to complete God's renovation process.

Everything Is Working Together for Your Good

Your PAIN is connected to their PROMISE. Don't give up right through here. GOD is allowing it all to work together for your good.

You Are Enough

If it doesn't fit, don't force it. Stop trying to force them to love you. Real love happens on its own. Let them go. YOU are ENOUGH. You matter to God. He is the ONLY one who can give you what no one else can.

Seek to First Understand

Don't expect others to understand who you are now, and where you are going. If they have not first understood where you have been.
#God'sOpinionofUIsWhatMatters

Be Careful How Your Keys Are Used

There is a reason that some doors are made with a Lock that you don't need a key to open. In case of a fire, you can make a quick escape without having to look for a key. That's the way God works. He will always give you a quick way of escape. It's your choice to exit or stay and possibly burn up waiting.

Humility Begins in The Heart

Sometimes we wonder why God would trust us with the "Hard Part" when it comes to the matters and conversations of the heart concerning others. Be humbled when others trust you enough to come to you. Don't take this lightly, and don't take it for granted. #Grateful2BeAbletoHelpSomeoneElse

Don't Miss Out

God will always send who we need and what we need at the time we need them. It's up to us to recognize it and receive it. Don't miss your blessing because it's not packaged the way you expect it be. It's not the packaging. It's what's on the inside that makes the difference. #Don'tMissOut

Unmask Your Truth

If you take your mask off and get to know you, I promise that this will be the best thing you ever do. Don't live your life pretending to "BE" whom you were not created to "Become."

Under but Not Buried

Being the "underdog" is sometimes a great position to be in. The one everyone "heard" about but really don't know. The one they all talked about, criticized, laughed at, and pushed away. God only used those people in your life for a season to Position You for Purpose. What they didn't know is that you would be "Under" but for a season, and that when God brings you "Over" it ALL, there will be no one to get the glory but Him. #It'sWorkingTogetherforUrGood

Positive Words Bring New Life

When you love or care about someone, it's so important to speak well of them, even and especially when they don't believe it. Your words have power. Use the power of your words to plant seeds of healing, encouragement, hope, and inspiration. Just because they say that they are "fine" or doing "well," this may not necessarily be the truth. It's easy to dress up the "Outside" when the "Inside" is dying.

No Matter What, Keep Trying

Don't ever feel embarrassed about what has happened to you in your life or what you are currently going through. Every test and every trial is designed to make you stronger and wiser, which will ultimately equip you to handle what God has waiting for you. Continue to walk toward your blessing no matter how long it takes...the journey will be worth it!

How Are You Loving Today?

Unconditional Love gives, is selfless, enhances, endures, forgives, communicates, understands, listens, builds up. *Conditional Love* is selfish, self-seeking, blames others, rejects responsibility, holds grudges. How are you loving today?

Action Speak Louder Than Words

Having unwavering faith will allow you to talk louder with your mouth closed. Give more with your heart open. Love more without expectations. Receive more when you take risks. Understand more with your eyes closed and reach for more, believing in the God who is the center and creator of it all.

Recalibrate Your Heart

If your words come from a tainted place (your heart), then you are better off keeping your mouth closed. Be careful not to let your tainted words cause someone to become *infected* instead of *affected*.

Who Are You?

Maturity is the ability to openly express your feelings to someone without expecting the same in return. Security is the ability to be you authentically and unapologetically without cause, even if at times that means standing alone. Knowing WHO you are and WHOSE you are makes all the difference.

How Are You Evolving?

Throughout life there will always be someone watching you. They may watch from a distance most of the time, never saying anything. Don't try and figure out the "whos" and "whys"; just make sure that they learn something positive from watching you, no matter whether your present condition is good or bad. Your position is key to their evolution. I hope I've helped someone evolve.

Don't Wait on "Them" Be "YOU"

Truth is, not everyone will love you; love anyway. Not everyone will appreciate you; give anyway. Not everyone will forgive you; forgive yourself and live anyway. Not everyone will listen to you; don't stop speaking the truth. Not everyone will acknowledge you; continue to remain present. Not everyone will embrace you; don't stop reaching out. Not everyone will compliment you; compliment yourself. Live your *Best Life Now,* because later may never come.

Free Your Mind

Mental health is so important. There is NOTHING wrong with getting counseling. There are so many "Beautiful" and "Handsome" broken people walking around who are silently dying on the inside.

Who Cares?

You will know how much someone really cares about you by the number of excuses they make when you really need them. Stop running to be a first responder to someone who has on their "Out of Service" light on when you need them.

You Can't Move Forward Walking Backwards

Don't miss your intended blessing worrying about the past; it is gone. Move forward to the greater blessing that God has awaiting you. The worst thing that you think could ever happen to you might turn out to be the best thing that ever happened to you.

Don't Settle

Don't allow your vision to become clouded, therefore, complicating the process of recognizing "The One" whom God has sent in your life. Don't allow your emotions, longings, and desires to be wanted, loved, and included lead you to settle for the bare "Minimum" when God is preparing the "Maximum" for You.

Don't Force It

You can't expect him to possibly love you if he is still trying to figure out how to love himself. You can't force a man to love you, especially when what he has seen or experienced has only been conditional.

He Loves You... Not

If the ONLY place he takes you is behind closed doors, he can't possibly love or care about you. A man who truly loves and cares about you wouldn't want to hide you; he would want the world to know and see YOU.

No Pretending Here

When you are truly confident in who you are, you will never have to pretend to be someone you are not just for people to recognize you.

It Had to Happen This Way

Don't be afraid to live in your "NOW" because others know the failures of your "PAST." No one can tell your story better than YOU. Come out of hiding; your story may help save someone's life.

Forgiveness Gives You Permission to Live

Stop allowing people to hold you hostage in "their" cage of unforgiveness and bitterness. Don't beat yourself up any longer. You have already apologized, and God has forgiven you. So, move on.

Keep Shining

You don't have to do "extra" to get "their" attention. Being authentically YOU should be enough. Never let anyone cause you to diminish your confidence to accommodate their comfort. You will never have to compete for what God already promised YOU…It's already Yours!

Heart of Stone

They will never feel your "true heart" concerning "them" as long as they have unresolved issues with you. Stop trying.

Stay Ready

It's in the stillness of these MOMENTS that GOD will speak. Make sure you are in a ready position to hear Him clearly. Don't be so anxious to move that you MISS what He is saying. He may be using this time to answer YOUR series of prayers all at ONCE... He is JUST that KIND of GOD.

Use What You Got

You will not be judged based on how much space you occupy, but by what you do with the space you've been given..."More" is not the same as "effective." It's hard to lead someone out of what you have not yet MASTERED.

Be Careful How You Climb

Don't allow your "come-up" be a result of another's "downfall." You will reap what you sow. The "neck" that you try and step on today just may be attached to the "back" of the same person whom you may need to carry you, when you fall tomorrow…#BeCareful

Perfectly Imperfect

No one is "perfect," stop pretending that you have it "all" together. It's okay to ask for help. Your "trial" today will add to another's "triumph" tomorrow.

God Is Worth the Wait

Moving forward is at times hard but necessary in order to receive all that God has for you. Waiting on God is never easy, but I promise it will be worth it. He heard your prayers and He will answer. Don't give up. Never settle for the bare minimum when God intended for you to obtain the maximum. Remain focused; you are almost there.

But Who Are You in Real Life?

Social networking enables a lot of people, who would otherwise in person be overlooked, to create the fantasy version of "WHO" they would like to be in "Real Life." Don't be so quick to fall for the sweet words and comments. These same people are really not "WHO" you think they are. When you are secure with YOU first, you will know the difference.

Slow Your Roll

Stop being so anxious to just be "In love" or have a relationship. The one that you are loving may not be God's best for you. Besides, you may only be loving or having a relationship with the "Representative" of that person; not the TRUE them.

Value What's In Your Hands

One should never become so familiar with a person or a situation that you ignore the changes that are happening around you. In the time of ignoring, you may miss out on something that may impact your life forever. Value what's in your hands, because God will remove it for good. This is not the year to play.

Trust

The moment you begin to believe in GOD beyond man's ability to believe in you, you can live a life of TRUE FREEDOM. If you want to experience all that God has for you, give Him your all with your eyes closed. Serve Him intentionally when no one is watching.

They Will Never Understand

There will be a time when people question the "hows" and "whys" of God's present uninterrupted blessings and favor in your life. Truth is, they will NEVER understand it because they were nowhere around when you were going through hell.

Rocessed For Purpose

If you have never been hurt, you wouldn't know what it felt like to heal. If you were never taken for granted, you wouldn't know what it felt like to be vulnerable. If you never opened your heart to someone who didn't appreciate nor deserve it, you wouldn't know what it felt like to be rejected. If you were never talked about, you wouldn't know what it felt like to be popular. The purpose of this process was designed to propel you into your destiny!
#ItWorked2getherForUrGood

What Matters Most

Material things can get lost, stolen, or even given away. But the most expensive gift that you can give to someone is a smile, a kind word of encouragement, a hug, or just a simple word of thanks to God for being who He is in your life and your family. Focus on what really matters. That which comes from the heart will last forever.

Right Size, Right Packaging

Be careful not to reject "the gift" because of its packaging. It just may be God's way of testing your faith while blessing you at the same time.

Be The TRUE You

People often work real hard at being a "Dressed-up" version of EMPTY. Be true to yourself and heal from the inside out. I promise you it will be worth it.

Blocked and Blessed

What they thought they were "BLOCKING" you from only created a greater way to "Escape"... Sometimes you just gotta tell God, thank you!

He Who Finds Me

God will replace the one who hurt, ignored, isolated, used, and rejected you with the one who will and is secure enough to fearlessly embrace, love, encourage, listen to, believe, and walk side by side with you. He who finds you will find a great thing.

Ready, Willing, and Waiting

You will never know how much they care about you until you stop caring about them. By then, it will be too late and wouldn't matter. Stop wasting time on someone who has no intentions. Life is too short. Let them go. God has someone waiting who is READY.

Best Is Better

Sometimes, what looks to be the WORST thing to happen in your life ends up being the BEST thing to ever happen to you... #WorkYourFaith

Break the Chain

Don't allow your childhood trauma to bleed on to your children. Get the help you need.

Let Him Perfect the Work

God never makes a mistake. He kept you here for a reason! Your work is not complete. Keep trusting and believing Him to perfect everything concerning You!

Keep On Moving

If they truly Love you, they will not only tell you but show you. If they want you to be a part of their life, they will invite you into it. You don't have to find a place to fit. If they really want you to know about them truthfully, they will tell you their whole story, not just part of it. If they truly trust you, it will be known by their response to you during their difficult moments, no matter how bad those moments get. If it doesn't fit, don't force it. Let it go. God has just created an escape for you.

Make Room

For EVERY person who has walked out of your life, God will send one better. Don't hold on to what's not holding on to you. Let them go so you will have room to receive your "BETTER."

Pace Yourself

One should strive daily to become an asset, rather than a hindrance, to someone else's growth. In a negative situation, a positive word goes a long way. Everyone's level of growth is different. Don't judge someone else because their growth does not match your expectation. #GodHastheFinalSay

How Is Your View?

Being authentic requires a certain level of transparency. How can one be transparent when wearing a mask is most comfortable? Truth is, a mask can hide the face but not the eyes. They are the windows to your soul. #Don'tFoolNobodyButYourself

Let God Upgrade You

God will remove certain people from your life to replace them with who and what is best for you. God will always upgrade you with what you deserve. They probably stopped liking you because of your honesty. Trust they haven't stopped watching you.

More than Enough

Gone are the days where "just enough" is all it takes. What you ignore, someone else is paying attention to. What you take for granted, someone else is willing to treasure. What you pretend not to see, someone else sees and is in awe. What you push away, someone else is wanting to hold close. Don't leave the door open for someone else to snatch your opportunity. It can all be gone in the blink of an eye.

Gift Giver

Think about giving yourself something that money can't buy: the gift of "RELEASE" and "GOODBYE" to the people and things that have merely been liabilities, emotionally and spiritually. I am making room for the ASSETS that have been waiting to trade places with you. #ReadytoReceive

Big Open Door

There is someone somewhere having a conversation about you. You don't have to beg for what GOD has already promised you. Stay the course; the door He is opening for you is way larger than the one that "they" are trying to keep closed.

Real Love

REAL LOVE embraces, endures, shelters, and protects. It communicates and comes in closer during difficult times and seasons. It doesn't run away during those times in silence. GOOD LOVE gives even when it hurts. STRONG LOVE builds unbreakable foundations. SENSITIVE LOVE helps you walk through the storm even when your legs are too weak to carry you. UNCONDITIONAL LOVE holds you through it ALL.

Who's Calling You?

They probably stopped liking you because of your honesty. Trust they haven't stopped watching you. The moment you realize that your "calling" is greater than what they "call" or think about you is when you will proceed with caution. Not everyone that says they love you really likes you. Some only love the part of you that serves them. Keep in mind, everyone who "calls" you don't really like you. They only entertain you because there is something you have that they "want." Don't give them what they "want," give them what they need. Give them "JESUS."

Net Watcher

Stop worrying about the Internet and worry about what's in YOUR "Net." What did you catch today?

Love Makes Things Happen

Some often want the finished product of what love "does" without first going through the process of yielding to it, building it, embracing it, refining it, sacrificing oneself for it, fighting for it, believing in it, and securing it on a sure and solid foundation. Long-lasting love will always cost you something; but it will be worth it.

P.O. Box 453
Powder Springs, Georgia 30127
www.entegritypublishing.com
info@entegritypublishing.com

www.ingramcontent.com/pod-product-compliance
Lightning Source LLC
LaVergne TN
LVHW020419070526
838199LV00055B/3665